Original title:
Winter's Frozen Whispers

Copyright © 2024 Creative Arts Management OÜ
All rights reserved.

Author: Lila Davenport
ISBN HARDBACK: 978-9916-94-586-5
ISBN PAPERBACK: 978-9916-94-587-2

Beneath the Silent Surface

Beneath the snow, where things are still,
Squirrels argue over acorn thrill.
The groundhog peeks, a furry sneak,
Whispers of spring make creatures freak.

Laughter echoes from icy trees,
While penguins slide with perfect ease.
A snowman's hat flies off in glee,
As rabbits hop like they're on spree.

Tales from the Frostbitten Woods

In the woods, the mice do skate,
On frosty ponds, it's quite the fate.
A deer slips down, gives quite a shout,
All the critters gather round to pout.

Chilly winds play tricks on their tails,
While the fox tries to tell some tales.
The owls hoot, "You'll catch a chill!"
But they laugh and dance, against their will.

The Dance of Snow and Silence

Snowflakes twirl like dancers bold,
In swirling patterns, stories told.
A bear wears shades, a real cool sight,
While rabbits hop in pure delight.

The trees sway gently, a frosty jig,
With squirrels joining, right up to the gig.
A snowball flies with gleeful zest,
As critters gather for the best fest.

Shivers of the Midnight Sky

The stars above, they twinkle bright,
While frosty air causes quite a fright.
A moose dons a scarf; what a view,
While penguins gather for hot chocolate brew.

The night critters chatter, full of cheer,
As laughter breaks through the chilly sphere.
They toast to warmth and winter plays,
While the moon giggles, through frosty rays.

Icy Breath of Night

Chilly winds begin to tease,
Tickling noses, making sneezes.
Snowflakes dance like tiny spies,
Making us look silly, oh my!

Hot cocoa's the only solution,
While snowflakes flurry in wild confusion.
With hats askew and mittens mismatched,
The frosty fun, nobody can hatch!

Frost-Painted Dreams

A snowman with a carrot nose,
His smile gives us colds and woes.
He wobbles as we throw a snowball,
With every hit, he starts to sprawl!

Sledding down the hill so fast,
With giggles echoing, we laugh and gasp.
We scatter like snowflakes, all around,
In this frozen circus, pure joy is found!

The Lullaby of Stillness

Under blankets, snug and warm,
We hear the crunch of snow, the charm.
Every step's a goofy dance,
As if the ice gave us a chance!

We slip and slide, a comic sight,
Each tumble turns into delight.
With frosty breath, we sing out loud,
Even the icicles seem very proud!

Beneath a Veil of White

Snowflakes twirl like ballerinas,
Spinning round on frozen arenas.
The dog leaps high, caught in mid-air,
Chasing snowballs without a care!

As branches bow from heavy loads,
We giggle at our awkward codes.
Every snowball fight, a silly game,
In this icy playground, we're never the same!

Welcome Silence of Snow

A plump bunny hops, oh what a sight,
Its fluffy tail makes everything bright.
It tumbles and rolls with a giggling sound,
While the snowflakes twirl all around.

A snowman grins with a carrot nose,
His stick arms waving as laughter grows.
But he melts a bit under the sun's ray,
And shouts, 'Not fair! It's my melting day!'

Echoing Through the Cold

A penguin slides with such glee,
Calling friends, 'Come slide with me!'
They zoom and spin, making a mess,
Then flop on ice, oh what bliss!

A moose in boots struts down the lane,
As squirrels laugh, 'He's a bit insane!'
With each awkward step, a belly laugh,
He takes a bow, 'I'm the winter's giraffe!'

Cold Embrace at Dusk

The trees wear coats all white and cozy,
As snowflakes giggle, feeling rosy.
A fox in a scarf looks quite refined,
As fellow critters fall behind.

A snowball fight sends flurries high,
One lands on a bird, oh me, oh my!
The bird just squawks, 'That's quite the toss!'
While friends all shout, 'You're the true boss!'

The Glistening Blanket

The world outside is dressed so neat,
With a layer that makes every walk feel sweet.
A cat in boots tries to prance,
But slips and spins in a snowy dance!

The sun peeks out, a warm fuzzy ray,
'Let's build a snow fort!' the kids say.
They gather the snow in a hurry and race,
Creating a kingdom in this frosty place!

Frosted Tides

A penguin slipped on icy ground,
Waved to a seal, who twirled around.
Attempting a dance, they fell in a heap,
In a frosty embrace, they started to weep.

Snowflakes laughed as they fluttered down,
Tickling the nose of a frostbitten clown.
He juggled snowballs, but oh what a mess,
As they splattered his pants in a snowy caress.

Tracing Shadows in Snow

A squirrel in boots skated with glee,
Chasing his tail, oh what a sight to see!
He tripped on a twig, flipped head over feet,
Landed right by where the snowballs compete.

A rabbit in spectacles tossed snow on a fox,
Who hid in a bush with an array of socks.
They played hide and seek in a snowy tableau,
With giggles and snickers as fast as the snow!

The Frosted Canvas

Brush strokes of snow on the cold winter scene,
A snowman wore shades, living like a queen.
He danced with the wind, in a flurry of laughs,
While children built castles, with sparkly drafts.

A carrot-nosed jester, capricious and spry,
Hopped from the park bench and flew through the sky.
He landed in snow, which sent him a-flying,
With giggles around him, no need for crying.

The Murmur of Snowy Pines

The pines began chuckling, their branches all swayed,
As squirrels in mittens began their escapade.
They tossed little pinecones like snowballs on cue,
Started a rumble, the whole forest knew!

A bear in a hat tried to join in the fun,
But slipped on the ice while he went for a run.
With laughter resounding, he rolled and he tumbled,
Through a grove of pine where the trees softly rumbled.

Chilled Verses

Snowflakes dance like silly fools,
They twirl around in frosty schools.
Hot cocoa spills, we slip and slide,
As penguins laugh, we take a ride.

Scarves wrapped tight, we look absurd,
Mittens mismatched, it's all unheard.
Snowball fights in a hapless fling,
Each chuckle brightens, makes us sing.

Velvet White Beneath Stars

Blankets of white, stars shining bright,
Snowmen wobble, what a sight.
Carrots for noses, arms made of sticks,
Who knew crafting was such a mix?

There's a crunch with every step,
I think I left my skills inept.
Slipping, sliding on ice so slick,
Now I'm a figure skater, quick!

Serene Frosted Pathways

Paths adorned with glittering frost,
Lost in laughter, at what cost?
A tumble here, a giggle there,
Snowflakes tickle, we feel the air.

Drifts piled high, a fort in sight,
Commanders of snow, oh what delight!
Snowball cats, we're on a quest,
In frosty realms, we're at our best.

Radiance of a Frozen Dawn

Morning breaks with sparkly sheen,
Finding boots where they have been.
Socks that match? Oh what a shame!
Let's embrace the goofy game.

Laughter echoes through the chill,
Building dreams on frosty hill.
With each fall, the fun will grow,
In this twinkling world, we glow.

Frost's Gentle Caress

The ground is slick, a skating rink,
I tried to walk, but boy, I stink!
My dog just laughs, I take a tumble,
He skips and hops, I land with a jumble.

Icicles dangle, like a frozen prize,
I try to catch one, oh, what a surprise!
It falls on my head, a chilly gift,
While neighbors laugh, my spirits lift.

The Sound of Snowfall

Snowflakes dance, they swirl and spin,
I try to catch one, but where to begin?
I make a snowman, he's looking quite grand,
Till he tips over; oh, wasn't that planned!

The world is hushed, a whispering hush,
But my nose is red, I start to blush.
My mittens are soggy, my boots full of snow,
I slip on the ice—don't let this show!

Echoes of the Icebound Night

Under the moon, the stars brightly beam,
I tell a joke, snowflakes team.
They don't laugh much, just freeze in the air,
But when I slip, they all seem to care!

My friends all gather, with hats oh so big,
They try to dance, but do the wrong jig.
A snowball's thrown, it hits with a splat,
"It's a fluffy attack!" I say with a chat.

Shivering Step on Crystal Paths

Each step I take feels like a game,
As I slip and slide, oh what a shame!
I chuckle and twirl, like a leaf in the breeze,
"Next time I'll bring a pair of skis!"

The cold nips my nose, I'm starting to groove,
I sing to the snow, trying to move.
The whole world chuckles, a merry delight,
As I dance with the frost, all through the night!

The Quiet Symphony of the Snowbound World.

Snowflakes dance with frosty grace,
They giggle as they fall in place.
The trees wear coats of purest white,
They shiver softly, what a sight!

Squirrels slip on icy paths,
Trying to escape the snowman's laughs.
Penguins wobble, full of cheer,
"Go ahead, we'll slide, not fear!"

Mailboxes wear a snowy hat,
While rabbits hop, then slip, then splat.
A hot cocoa spills in delight,
As snowmen plot to have a snowball fight.

The moon peeks in, a curious guest,
As snowflakes whisper, "We are the best!"
With cheeks all rosy, all out of breath,
They raise a cup, "To fun, not death!"

Chill of Silence

The silence falls, a frosty tune,
Bunnies hop beneath the moon.
Icicles play a jingling song,
But owls say, "Hey, this feels wrong!"

Snowmen stare with carrot noses,
While the winds sing jokes in poses.
A sudden gust makes hats take flight,
"Oh dear, where'd my beanie bite?"

Fluffy clouds toss snow around,
While yodeling penguins joy abound.
And laughter echoes through the trees,
As children shout, "We'll catch the breeze!"

The frozen ground shakes with glee,
As squirrels quip, "Come watch me ski!"
In this chill, no need for frowns,
Just winter fun in snow-filled towns!

Frigid Echoes

Icicles chime in frosty air,
While froggie says, "Come on, let's dare!"
Snow drifts whisper from the hills,
"Join us now, we've got the thrills!"

Penguins strut with flair and spice,
Waddling snug, oh, isn't that nice?
Boys and girls in snow gear loud,
Launching snowballs—oh, so proud!

A snowman winks, his nose ablaze,
While all around, the snowflakes blaze.
Carrots giggle on frosty heads,
"Who will win? Place your bets!"

As laughter echoes down the lane,
Slipping up, they try again.
In this season of icy cheer,
Joy abounds—far and near!

Snowflakes' Secret Serenade

Tiny flurries fall like dreams,
They whisper soft, or so it seems.
A snowman plots a prank so sly,
"Let's loosen up and let it fly!"

Twirling round, some kids now trip,
While hot cocoa takes a sip.
Penguins laugh with merry cheer,
Snowball fights are drawing near!

Icicles sway, a magical ballet,
With frosty critters joining play.
A snow angel flaps with delight,
"Don't get stuck or lose the fight!"

Cheery snowflakes prance around,
Their giggles twinkling, joy unbound.
In this season so absurd,
Life's a laugh that's never blurred!

The Poetry of a Frosty Dawn

The sun peeks out, a cheeky grin,
And all the snowflakes start to spin.
A squirrel dances, not a care,
While icicles dangle from a chair.

The world is white, a frosty quilt,
With chilly air, our noses wilt.
Yet penguins laugh as if they know,
That warmth returns with the next show.

Unseen Currents in the Chilling Breeze

The breeze has jokes, it whispers low,
Tickling cheeks as it comes and goes.
I laugh with mittens, what a charade!
While snowmen gossip, they've got it made.

The rooftops glisten, quite the sight,
But I can't help but feel a bit light.
With every gust, I spin and sway,
As frostbite's villain steals my bouquet.

Secrets in the Sparkling Twilight

Dusk descends with glittering cheer,
Snowflakes chuckle, giving a jeer.
Twinkling lights in icy display,
Mice slyly plot for snacks, hooray!

Under the glow, the shadows dance,
Cats play tag, an icy romance.
The moon winks down, it's quite sublime,
While frosty critters mime in rhyme.

Melodies of a Frozen Stream

The brook is frozen, but what a tune!
Cracking ice sings a funny croon.
Fish are plotting without a clue,
While otters slide, oh what a view!

Bubbles form like laughter, bright,
As turtles shuffle in sheer delight.
Nature giggles, frosty and round,
In this chilly realm, joy is found.

Silken Threads of Frost

Tiny flakes of chilly cheer,
Dancing down without a fear.
Snowmen grin with carrot nose,
Where's my scarf? Oh, there it goes!

Snowball fights and snowman games,
Sleds that flew, oh what a shame!
Frosty breath in playful squeals,
Underneath these frosty wheels.

Icicles hang like toothy fangs,
Watch your step, and hear the clangs.
Laughter echoes through the night,
In this cold, we find delight.

So grab your mittens, let's be bold,
In this chill, we'll laugh till old.
Sipping cocoa, what a dream!
In snowy fun, we're quite the team!

A Pale Stillness

A quiet shiver fills the air,
Noses red, and frosty hair.
Sleds as ships on pillows white,
Let's set sail, oh, what a sight!

Pine trees dressed in winter's best,
Squirrels running for a nest.
"Did you see that?" someone shouts,
As snowflakes play, there are no doubts.

Hot soup warms the chilly toes,
Look out, here comes another dose!
With snowball fights much like a war,
Giggles echo, hear them soar.

So let's embrace this chilly glee,
With laughter shared, and friendly spree.
Crafting fun beneath the grey,
In this season, let's all play!

Shadows in the Snowfall

Shadows dance on soft white ground,
Laughter bubbling all around.
Snowflakes whisper silly tales,
Of penguins who wear suits and veils.

Snowmen do the cha-cha slide,
While cold wind seems to take a ride.
Sleds crash with a comical boom,
Snow-kissed cheeks in winter's room.

Hot cocoa spills, oh what a mess,
"Is that marshmallow or my dress?"
Giggles echo, crisp and bright,
As shadows play in fading light.

Grab your gloves, it's time to race,
In this frost, we'll find our place.
Snowflakes giggle in delight,
In this chill, we'll spark the night!

Frozen Tales Under Moonlight

Under the moon's soft silver glow,
Frosty figures start to flow.
Snowflakes fall with playful ease,
Telling stories in the breeze.

A penguin in a tie appears,
Spinning tales that spark our cheers.
"Did you hear about the prancing deer?"
With every tale, a chuckle near.

Snowflakes twirl like dancers grand,
Sliding cups of cocoa in hand.
Noses pink from the breezy bite,
Tell your tales, it feels so right.

So gather 'round, don't freeze away,
In frosty fun we'll laugh and play.
Under the stars, let's make our stand,
In this cold, we'll grow so grand!

Nightfall's Frosted Breath

Cold air tickles noses, oh what fun,
Snowflakes dance like fairies, one by one.
A snowman with a carrot, looking quite grand,
Waving to the penguins, in a frosty band.

Hot cocoa smiles, marshmallows afloat,
Sipping in puffer jackets, what a coat!
Sneaky snowballs fly, a fluffy delight,
Kids giggle and scatter, a comical sight.

The moon peeks out, a silver shadow,
While snow angels wave from their bed of white meadow.

A frosty comedy, nature's great show,
With laughter and shivers, oh how they glow!

As night deepens, the icy chill play,
Feet slipping and sliding, in a humorous way.
In this playful world, where giggles are cast,
Each moment a treasure, winter's hilarity lasts.

The Music of a Quiet Landscape

Whispers of the snowflakes, a gentle hum,
Hushed giggles echo, like beats of a drum.
Sledding down hills, with a cheer and a shout,
Who knew that slipping could be such a rout?

Icicles hang like teeth from eaves,
Watch out for the drip, or it might be leaves!
A snowball fight brews, like a perfect storm,
Puffs of white chaos keeping us warm.

Frosty rooftops make for a splendid scene,
While penguins in parkas think they're quite keen.
Snowmen gossip, with carrots for noses,
Sharing all secrets the cold finally exposes.

The calm might be quiet, yet silliness plays,
As snowballs collide and create funny pais.
Nature's own symphony, a wintertime spree,
Brings laughter and warmth, for you and for me.

Caught in a Snowy Dream

A soft fluffy blanket covers the town,
Kids tumble and tumble, they fall down.
Their laughter erupts, a sound so divine,
As adults shake heads at their snowy design.

Snowflakes pirouette in a whimsical dance,
Icicles drop down, like a cold trance.
With mittens askew and scarves out of place,
It's hard not to chuckle at each rosy face.

Sleds zoom downhill, like rockets in flight,
With grace of a penguin, they take off in spite.
Plowing through drifts that rise up like walls,
The snow seems to giggle as everyone falls.

In dreams of snowmen and chocolaty treats,
The cocoa is flowing, life's simple beats.
With snow piling higher, it's hard to resist,
Laughter and joy in each frosty twist.

Crystal Silence

Under shining stars, the ground's tucked in tight,
The world's a little hushed, not a creature in sight.
Snow, like soft pillows, draped over the land,
Whispers of frost tickling each little hand.

Children shiver and giggle, a sight to behold,
With cheeks like ripe apples, glimmers of gold.
A snowball's a friend, with a squishy embrace,
A face full of laughter—oh what a race!

The trees wear their dresses of glistening white,
While squirrels are plotting their cheeky delight.
Their antics amusing, as they leap and they bound,
In this frosty world, where fun can be found.

So here in this realm, where the quiet is bright,
Let the humor of crystals bring warmth to the night.
For even in silence, laughter sings free,
In the magic of frost, just you wait and see!

Echos in the Icicle Forest

In the forest, ice jokes glide,
Icicles laugh, there's no need to hide.
Snowmen debate in a witty brawl,
Who wears the best hat? They've got it all.

A squirrel tries to slide with grace,
But faceplants hard, oh what a case!
The trees chuckle, branches in glee,
Who knew winter was such a spree?

Birds in scarves serenade the sun,
While rabbits hop, oh what fun!
Goblins of snow, prancing around,
In a frosty, chuckling playground.

So grab your mittens, let's join the fun,
In a land where icicles wink and run.
With giggles and jiggles manifold,
These frozen echoes are pure gold.

The Secret Life of a Snowflake

A snowflake twirls with grand ambition,
Each landing soft, a silent mission.
But wait! The ground feels warm and bright,
"Oops," it shrieks, "I wasn't meant for flight!"

Disguised as fluff, it wears a crown,
Waltzing softly, then falling down.
"Not so fast!" yells a busy bee,
"Who knew winter had such a spree?"

A snowflake slip in a hot cocoa mug,
Leaves the snowman with a sarcastic shrug.
"Don't melt away, you fancy flake,
At least stay frosty for goodness' sake!"

So twirl and twist in this chill dance,
Where every flake has a snowflake chance.
In the warmth of a laugh, we all gauge,
The secret of snow is pure mirth on stage.

Threads of Frostwoven Dreams

In a land stitched with frosty seams,
Chasing threads of ridiculous dreams.
Snowmen model in runway shows,
Wearing carrot noses, striking poses.

A cat in mittens sits on a throne,
While snowball trades make headlines known.
"Did you hear how Slippery Joe fell?"
The icicles chime with a jolly yell.

A penguin on skates, just lost its flair,
Spins and tumbles, but has not a care.
"Did you see that?" the other birds cry,
"Flapper extraordinaire, oh my, oh my!"

So gather round in this chill delight,
Where snowflakes giggle through day and night.
With threads of laughter woven tight,
Let's dance in dreams 'til morning light.

Chasing Shadows in a Snowy Veil

In shadows deep, the snowflakes plot,
To tease the sun in a daring hot shot.
With a wink and a nudge, they dance and sway,
Chasing their silhouettes, come what may.

The rabbits giggle, hopping about,
While squirrels shout, "What's this fuss about?"
Snowballs roll, a comedy act,
Watch out for the sneezes, that's a fact!

Icicles drip down with a grin so sly,
"Catch me if you can!" they taunt the sky.
And the air is filled with giggles galore,
As we chase in the snow, forevermore.

So take a step in this frosty shroud,
Where shadows play and laughter's loud.
In this veil of snow, let's embrace this spree,
Chasing our dreams in gleeful jubilee.

Chill in the Air

The air is crisp, my nose is red,
I can't feel my toes, I should've fled.
The snowflakes dance like they just don't care,
While I sip cocoa with marshmallows to spare.

The squirrels wear coats, looking quite dapper,
As they plot their escape, oh what a caper!
The snowmen grin with their carrot-y smiles,
I wonder how long they'll last in these miles.

The laughs come easy, the cheeks turn bright,
Snowball fights ignite, it's pure delight.
But watch for the slip, oh I take a dive,
Rolling like a snowball, am I still alive?

So let's embrace, this frosty fun,
With giggles and snow, oh we've just begun!
Let's bask in the freeze, till the daylight peeks,
And we'll dream of warmth for a few more weeks!

Secrets Beneath the Snow

Beneath the white, secrets lie deep,
Like snowmen's plans for a midnight creep.
The rabbits conspire, oh what a sight,
Hopping about with glee, oh what a fright!

The flakes keep falling, but do they conspire?
Whispering softly, igniting the fire.
They cover all mischief with a soft white shroud,
While I chase my cat, tangled up in the crowd!

The children are cunning, they laugh and they leap,
But somehow my nose got stuck in a heap!
I hear the snow giggling, can you believe?
While I'm trying to dig my poor self to reprieve.

So let's share a secret, just you and me,
On what really hides beneath the cold spree.
It's laughter and joy, where the chill likes to dwell,
Wrapped up in snow, life's a glimmering spell!

The Silence of Icebound Dreams

Dreams laid on ice like a thick frozen cream,
Slipping and sliding, oh what a theme!
I tiptoe with caution, like a stealthy ninja,
But gravity laughs as I slip like a pinza.

The trees wear white robes, quite regal they sway,
As I try to dance, but the ground steals my play.
With a plop and a splash, I'm a snowman's friend,
Digging for dignity, will this ever end?

The silence is loud, it tickles my ear,
As snowflakes bombard me without any fear.
The chill wraps around me, a frosty old hug,
While I'm busy thinking, "Is this just a bug?"

So here's to the dreams that slip through the frost,
Where laughter is found, and nothing is lost.
I'll wrap myself in whimsy till spring calls my name,
And remember this winter, forever the same!

Echoes of the Frosted Hearth

The hearth is aglow, with warmth in the air,
But the cookies have vanished! Oh, what a scare!
The echo of laughter fills every nook,
While we chase down the crumbs, like a new page in a book.

The cats lay sprawled, plotting their snack,
While we tell silly tales, and laughter we stack.
Hot cocoa spills, but we giggle instead,
As the mugs tumble over, and chaos is fed.

The snow swirls outside, but in here it's bright,
As we dance like fools in the dim candlelight.
With marshmallow secrets and playful delight,
We bask in the echoes, till it turns into night.

So gather around, with stories to share,
With friends by the fire, and no need to beware.
In the frost of the moment, we'll cherish the glee,
Echoing memories, just you wait and see!

Murmurs of a Frigid Moon

The moon wears a scarf, quite tightly bound,
It shivers and shakes on the icy ground.
An owl asks it why it's quaking so,
The moon just grins, says, "Just go with the flow!"

Snowflakes giggle like they're in a race,
They tumble and twist in a dazzling chase.
A penguin slides by on a beaming spree,
"Hey folks, this chill's just fab as can be!"

The stars give a wink, they're feeling spry,
They twinkle with laughter up high in the sky.
A rabbit hops in, his ears cold but bold,
"Anyone want to join me? I'm peddling gold!"

So let's make a toast with warm mugs of brew,
To the joys of the frost and the fun we pursue.
In the hush of the night, let's crank up the cheer,
For those funny frigid whispers we hold dear.

Frosty Breaths of Forgotten Lore

In the woods, tales freeze in the icy air,
A squirrel recounts them, a grin hard to bear.
He stutters and sputters, all bundled in fluff,
"Did you hear the one 'bout the cat? It's quite rough!"

The snowman dances, his buttons all wrong,
He twirls and he shimmies to a jazzy song.
He slips on a patch of slick shiny ice,
"Oh dear, not again! I better think twice!"

The winds carry whispers, oh what a squeal,
They tease and they tease, makes you spin like a wheel.
A polar bear giggles, feeling oh-so spry,
"Why not do ballet? Just give it a try!"

In this frosty realm, we chuckle and play,
Sharing tales of mishaps that brighten the gray.
So when the chill comes, let laughter ignite,
In the tapestry of frost, we'll find pure delight.

The Crystal Garden of Silence

A garden of frost with a sprinkle of cheer,
Where snowmen gossip, their secrets unclear.
A bunny hops by, in boots two sizes wide,
"I can't feel my feet, but who needs them to glide?"

Ice crystals giggle on branches all around,
With whispers of joy in a silent sound.
A hedgehog complains that it's too cold to eat,
"Where's my hot cocoa? This chill feels like defeat!"

The snowflakes all play hide and seek on the grass,
"Tag, you're it!" they chirp, as they swirl and they pass.
A turtle in mittens joins in on the fun,
"I'm slow, but I've got jokes—let's get this done!"

So here in this garden of glimmer and glee,
We'll dance through the frost, let the laughter run free.
In the heart of the chill, we'll warm up the night,
With silly little stories that just feel so right.

Lament of the Icy Stars

Oh the icy stars twinkle in clusters and clumps,
With laughter and giggles, they bounce like little bumps.
One tumbles and fumbles through the midnight haze,
"Watch out below! I'm coming in a daze!"

The big bear up there yawns with quite a flair,
"I'll catch a snowflake, if it dares to dare!"
As the comets zoom by with their sparkles and trails,
They giggle through the cosmos, sharing silly tales.

Some polar bears waltz beneath the moon's glow,
While frosty dinosaurs start to put on a show.
"Come join our dance! We've got moves like no other,"
"Just don't step on my toes!" yells the tyrant's mother.

So when night falls down with a chill and a shout,
We'll revel in laughter, that's what it's about.
For the icy stars here always know how to play,
And keep the fun rolling on a chilly display.

Beneath the Veil of Snowflakes

Snowflakes dance like tiny sprites,
They land on noses, oh so bright.
A snowman's hat is slightly askew,
He looks like he just had a brew.

Hot cocoa spills on my new mittens,
I swear those marshmallows have kittens.
Sledding down hills with squeals of glee,
Just pray that tree doesn't notice me!

Frosty air tickles my chin,
I trip on my scarf—where to begin?
Footprints lead where it all began,
To the nearest hot dog stand!

Laughter echoes through the trees,
As we race against the cold breeze.
Every slip earns a joyous shout,
Who knew fun could be this sprout?

The Lullaby of Cold Winds

Cold wind howls, what a melody,
It sings of frosty calamity.
A penguin in the park sings a tune,
While squirrels choreograph under the moon.

Snowballs fly like cannonballs do,
They always land where it's not meant to.
Each throw ends with a surprised little face,
And giggles erupt in the coldest of places.

Tiny rabbits think they're all stars,
Dashing through drifts like bizarre midnights cars.
Their fluffy little tails twitch with pride,
Who knew such fluff could glide and slide?

Then comes the sun, with a cheeky grin,
Melting snowmen, where do we begin?
A puddle forms, and what do we see?
The ghost of a snowman dancing with glee!

Glistening Tales of the Frozen Realm

Icicles hang like crystal swords,
Stalactites waiting for winter's hoards.
But slip, and oh!—what a sight,
Down goes the warrior, in pure delight.

Snowy trails are for the brave,
But watch your step or miss the wave.
A playful pup dashes with glee,
Then finds himself stuck to a tree!

Gloves on feet make a funny show,
Someone's rolled into that fluffy snow.
With a hearty laugh, they rise once more,
Only to slip and repeat the score.

Look, a hot air balloon made of snow!
A whimsical sight, but oh no, oh no!
Up it goes with a squeaky cheer,
It's winter circus, everyone's here!

Hushed Footprints on White Blankets

Footprints zigzag like a mad dance,
Leading to mischief and snowy romance.
What is that? A tap-dancing bear?
Or was it just my brother's hair?

Snowflakes fall with a gentle plop,
Landing on heads like a cherry hop.
Each giggle bursts like a balloon,
As they stick to hats, a frosty monsoon.

Hot hands from mittens, what a sight!
They wave goodbye in the frosty night.
A snowball fight breaks out with glee,
Who knew snow could be so free?

Finally, we collapse in a heap,
Dreaming of cookies and warmth—and sheep.
Just a day in this chilly fair,
With footprints leading everywhere!

Shards of Crystal Light

In the air, a frosty bite,
Snowflakes dance in pure delight.
Socks are damp, out of sight,
Chasing snowballs is a delight.

Icicles hang, a pointy threat,
Slip on ice? Not done just yet!
Laughter echoes, oh what a bet,
Someone's face, an icy net!

Snowmen built with silly hats,
Chubby cheeks and sneaky cats.
Those little snowflakes, oh how they spat,
Snowball fights—the best of chats!

Sledding down a hill, so grand,
Flying high, yet losing land.
A tumble here, a startled band,
Rolling snow and looking bland!

Whispering Pines in the Cold

Pine trees whisper tales of chill,
Dressed in white, they laugh at will.
Branches droop from frozen thrill,
Nature's joke, a frosty spill.

Squirrels in coats, they race the breeze,
Finding nuts underneath the freeze.
They're busy now with such great ease,
Planning tricks—oh, how they tease!

Frosty windows, breath like steam,
Rumors spread of snowman dreams.
They roll in balls, or so it seems,
Eyes like buttons, laughter beams!

Hot cocoa spills from mugs around,
Marshmallows dance, they float, they bound.
All this fun, and yet we've found,
Snowball fights can't be outdone!

Frostbitten Memories

Jackets zipped, we trudge along,
But one brave soul breaks into song.
Pants all wet, but still they're strong,
Memories made where we belong.

Frozen fingers, a silly dance,
Tumbling down, we take the chance.
Hot chocolate added to the prance,
We spill it all for a few laughs' glance!

Waving to cars while making snow,
Finding paths where snowflakes blow.
Slipping, sliding, hear the "whoa!"
No worries here, just laugh and show!

As shadows grow and daylight fades,
Our snowman glows—yes, we have made.
We'll treasure this in sunshine shades,
And video clips of our crusades!

Ghosts of Frostbite

The ghosts of frost, they come alive,
With icy jests, they love to thrive.
Chattering teeth, they can't deprive,
Of silly games, we'll all survive!

Surrounded by snow, I hear a giggle,
One brave snowman starts to wiggle.
As plops of snow begin to jiggle,
Our frozen fun's a cheerful wiggle!

Frosty faces all aglow,
Adventures lead where laughter flows.
Who can stack the highest snow?
With funny hats, we steal the show!

Frostbite ghosts tell tales so grand,
With frosted mugs held in hand.
Their stories, odd and slightly bland,
Bring warmth to chill across our land!

Gleaming in White

The snowflakes dance like tiny clowns,
They tickle noses, and tumble down.
They stick to mittens, give quite a fright,
As kids go sliding in pure delight.

A snowman grins with a carrot nose,
He wobbles slightly, then promptly doze.
With buttons missing and eyes askew,
He dreams of spring—oh, if only knew!

Snowball battles break out in glee,
While snowdrifts whisper their winter decree.
A sled on the hill gives a joyful shout,
But careful now, don't knock someone out!

Hot cocoa waiting, marshmallows afloat,
With giggles that thrum in a warm little boat.
So raise your mugs, with laughter so bright,
In a land where everything sparkles in white!

Threads of a Frozen Hearth

The fire crackles with a cozy hum,
While socks on heads make everyone glum.
A pot of soup starts doing a jig,
Reminding us all, dancing's not big!

The cat on the rug looks so perplexed,
His peaceful nap now completely vexed.
He swats at shadows on the frosty floor,
As if he's thinking, 'What's there to explore?'

Scarves are tangled, and hats mislaid,
An ensemble fashion that's not well played.
Snowflakes try to sneak through the door,
But we chase them off with a playful roar!

The furnace wheezes, creaks like an old man,
While kids plot mischief whenever they can.
The hearth's warm glow and laughter ignite,
In a tapestry woven of comical plight.

Echoing in the Stillness

Amidst the silence, a sneeze breaks free,
Echoing loudly in the quite snowy spree.
An army of jackets, scarves, and some mitts,
Trot down the lane, in their higgledy fits.

A cheeky dog rolls in piles of snow,
His joyous spins steal the show, you know!
He races past, a furry little blur,
Chasing his tail with a wintry slur.

Children stack snow in an ol' fashion way,
To build a tower, come join the fray!
But just one nudge, and oh what a sight,
A lovely white pile, they tumble in fright!

As twilight falls, the night claims its prize,
With lamps glowing golden like stars in disguise.
Laughter echoes through the cool, crisp air,
As magic dances, with fun everywhere!

A Winter's Solitary Song

A lone figure with boots, shuffling along,
Sings to the sky, a hilarious song.
With each little slip, there's laughter so bright,
As they tumble and roll, a comical sight!

Snowflakes stick to their cheeks like glue,
Creating a mask that's quite sticky too.
With a grand flourish, they wave to the trees,
Who giggle and sway in the shivering breeze.

The porch is adorned with lights twinkling wide,
While frozen icicles dance in their pride.
A snow globe scene of an ending delight,
As a snowman wonders, 'Is it day or night?'

So let us embrace this frosty old jest,
Wrapped in our blankets, feeling so blessed.
With snowmen and giggles, the cold melts away,
In this icy kingdom where we gleefully play!

Silence Wrapped in Snow

A snowman fell and took a dive,
He lost his hat, but still felt alive.
With carrot nose and eyes of coal,
He danced around, a jolly soul.

The squirrels skated on frozen ponds,
With tiny boots and fluffy fronds.
They laughed so hard, they forgot the cold,
Their winter antics, a sight to behold.

The flakes giggled as they came down,
Covering all with a soft white gown.
They tickled noses, they swept the ground,
In this frosty place, joy can be found.

And in the hush, a snowball fight,
Everyone joining, what a delight!
With laughter echoing, the air so bright,
Nothin' beats fun on a winter night.

Dances of the Winter Ghost

A ghost in white, so soft and light,
Could not find warmth, try as he might.
He twisted and turned in a silly jig,
While children laughed at his frozen gig.

With chilly breaths, he tried to sing,
But all that came was a blustery fling.
He tripped on ice and landed flat,
A comical scene, as soft as a cat.

The trees shook hands, but only with snow,
Their branches creaking, putting on a show.
As he danced and pranced in the cold air,
The winter ghost giggled at the fair.

With each silly step, the flakes took flight,
In the glow of the moon, everything's bright.
The ghost swirled 'round with frosty grace,
Winter's the stage for laughter's embrace.

The Quieting of the World

Once the leaves waved goodbye with cheer,
A blanket of white began to appear.
The ground took a snooze, so soft and deep,
While the world wrapped itself for a long sleep.

But in all that hush, a sound did arise,
A penguin slipped, much to our surprise.
With a wink and a laugh, he shimmed and slid,
In a line of friends, they all did a bid.

The whispers of snow caught in a breeze,
Tickled the toes of the big oak trees.
Together they chuckled, all quieted still,
In this frosty wonder, we found such thrill.

And though the world lay in slumber's kiss,
Laughter rang out, not a syllable missed.
For in the soft glow, all magic swirled,
The funniest times in this quiet world.

Echoes of a Frosty Heart

The ice cracked loud, a startling sound,
As frosty hearts danced on frozen ground.
With giggles and grins, they twirled around,
In the chill of the air, joy did abound.

Two penguins waddled, a comical sight,
Chasing each other 'til the fall of night.
They spun and they flopped, oh, what a show,
In a flurry of feathers, their hearts stole the glow.

The icicles dangled, like teeth with a smile,
While the rabbits leapt and frolicked a while.
A bashful snowflake floated by too,
Saying, "Tag, you're it!" as it landed anew.

With echoes of laughter, the night wore on,
Under starlit skies, till the break of dawn.
In this frost-kissed realm, we'll hold it dear,
For the magic of mirth brings us all cheer.

Serene Frost's Embrace

The snowman's carrot nose is slightly askew,
He looks quite surprised at the view.
A squirrel in a scarf dashes past,
Chasing a snowflake too quick to last.

The frozen pond's a wobbly stage,
Where ducks play ice-skates, quite the rage.
A snowball fight breaks out with glee,
As laughter echoes, wild and free.

Chilly cheeks and frosty toes,
Underneath the igloo, a secret snows.
Hot cocoa spills on the snowman's hat,
Now he's a fancy, chocolaty brat!

When spring arrives, they'll have a laugh,
Of winter's games, a silly half.
But for now, let the mischief flow,
In this chilly, whimsical show!

Breath of the Arctic

The penguin slid down the frosty hill,
With a clumsy twist and a comical thrill.
Snowflakes giggle as they land,
On a polar bear with a snowball band.

An owl wears glasses, quite the sight,
Reading a book by a candlelight.
The seal is teaching a dog how to dance,
As the flopping and sliding puts everyone in a trance.

Footprints lead in looping lines,
While bunnies play tag among the pines.
They hop and giggle, too wild to see,
The whirl of joy in the snowy spree.

As night falls bright with stars aglow,
The magic of laughter begins to grow.
In this frosted realm of silly delight,
Everyone's a jester, joy takes flight!

Frostbound Reflections

A moose in skates wobbles to the rink,
With each graceful fall, the kids all blink.
While icicles form on the fence post's tip,
A crafty raccoon joins the fun with a flip.

The chimney smoking is wafting sweet pies,
As kids roll in snow, sharing mischievous lies.
The icicles drip like glistening beads,
While squirrels play poker amidst snowy seeds.

Snow forts stand tall, a fortress of glee,
With secret tunnels for escape, you see?
Giggling gophers revel in cheer,
As snowflakes whisper shenanigans near.

With cheerful hearts, the cold can't bite,
As laughter dances in the pale moonlight.
Every freeze brings a quirky delight,
In this frosty land of playful flight!

Echoes in the Glimmering Snow

The snowflakes twirl like confetti in air,
As bunnies have tea in their snow-laden lair.
A polar bear dons a pink winter hat,
While a wise old owl just chuckles at that.

Children sled down hills in tandem delight,
Their giggles echoing into the night.
A snow fort named "Fort Giggle" stands tall,
With snowball artillery—take that, snowball!

Squirrels make angels in the slushy white,
While snowmen play chess 'neath the moonlight bright.
The cozy winds carry tales so absurd,
Like a cat's snowball dance, we all heard.

With icicles dripping like laughter so sweet,
Nature joins in on the funny winter treat.
Echos of joy stay bundled in tow,
In this frozen realm, where cheer always glows!

Frigid Caresses

The snowflakes dance, with silly grace,
Tickling noses, a frosty embrace.
Icicles hang, like frozen spears,
Laughing at winter, and all its fears.

Sleds go flying, through frostbitten air,
With kids laughing loud, without a care.
The snowman grins, his carrot askew,
Oh, the chilly chaos, in a sparkling view.

Hot cocoa spills, on mittens aglow,
As snowballs fly, in a frigid show.
Giggles erupt, with each icy blast,
Who knew frozen fun could go so fast?

Yet snug in blankets, we sip on our tea,
While snowbanks build up, as high as a spree.
Outside the chill reigns, but in here we stay,
With laughter and warmth on this frosty day.

Shimmering Dreams of Ice

Glittering crystals on rooftops sit,
A fashion show for snowflakes, oh what a hit!
The frost-tipped trees wear their sparkly crowns,
While squirrels in jackets parade through the towns.

Penguins on ice, in a colossal slide,
Slide into puddles, oh what a ride!
With flippers flapping, they take to the seas,
While polar bears dream of warm summer breeze.

The snowball fight is on, oh watch those throws,
Like ninja turtles in puffy white clothes!
Laughter erupts with each buddy's fall,
Who knew frozen fun could be such a brawl?

And when the sun sets, the laughter will linger,
With frostbitten fingers, and warmth on a singer.
Nestled in beds, we dream of the grace,
Of shimmering patches that blanket the place.

Nature's Frozen Melody

The wind hums a tune, a frosty delight,
While trees sway gently, dressed all in white.
Icicles jingle, as if in a band,
Nature's own symphony, under snow's hand.

A penguin's waddle brings much joyful cheer,
As frosty conditions are truly sincere.
With snowflakes fluttering, like tiny shy mice,
They leap from the heavens, and shimmer like spice.

Fresh tracks in the snow, oh what a treat,
A dog takes a tumble, with four spinning feet!
Bounding through drifts like a furry delight,
We laugh at their antics, what a whimsical sight!

So let's raise a toast, to this chilly affair,
With mugs full of warmth, in the frosty air.
Nature's a joker, with moments to spare,
And through all the laughter, it's hard not to care.

The Cradle of Solitude

A blanket of white wraps the world in still,
Cozy and quiet, it gives a chill.
The lone snowy owl hoots a soft tune,
Under pale stars, and the gleaming moon.

Under the stars, the snowflakes fall,
A silent parade, oh, they seem to call.
The critters are quiet, in their frostbitten homes,
While the season of laughter in stillness now roams.

Hot tea in hand, we chuckle and wink,
At the snowman stacked high, who can barely think.
With carrot dug out, oh what a face,
Nature's comedies in this quiet place.

As night wraps its cloak, and silence is deep,
We whisper our secrets, while others still sleep.
In the cradle of solitude, we find joy's embrace,
And giggles erupt in this very still space.

Midnight's Chill

The moonbeams dance on ice, oh dear,
My nose is red, and so is my beer.
Snowflakes giggle as they land in my hair,
I see my breath like dragons everywhere.

Socks are mismatched, not a single pair,
Slipping and sliding, I haven't a care.
Warmed by hot cocoa, I take a sweet sip,
But it spills on my lap, oh what a trip!

Frosty the snowman, where are your eyes?
He looks quite puzzled, oh what a surprise.
His carrot nose seems to be on the run,
Chasing the squirrels, oh, this is such fun!

Snowball fights in my backyard so grand,
But I missed my target, I hit Uncle Stan.
He laughed and retaliated in full swing,
Next thing I know, I'm the snowman's king!

The Tapestry of Ice

The layers of frost on my windowpane,
Look like a beauty mark, but drive me insane.
I tried to scrape it, but slipped on my foot,
Landed in snow, now I'm covered up to my boot.

Icicles dangle like frozen popsicles,
While I try to catch them, slipping like miracles.
My dog barks loud at the creeping snow,
As if it's the enemy, putting on a show.

Hot soup on the stove, bubbling with glee,
But I dropped the spoon, now it's hunting me!
It's chasing my feet, oh what a wild sight,
Maybe I'll just stick to cereal tonight.

As I trudge through the snow, oh such a delight,
I trip on a branch and give it a fright.
With laughter around me, winter's a blast,
Even if my pants are now wet to the last!

Shimmering Secrets of Solitude

The stars are twinkling, or maybe it's frost,
They wink at me, saying, 'You're not so lost.'
I'm bundled up tight, feeling quite the sight,
Like a marshmallow squished, oh what a plight!

Sipping my cocoa with laughter and cheer,
My cat is plotting a wintertime sneer.
He leaps through the drifts with all of his might,
Only to land in a snowdrift, what a fright!

The fireplace crackles with stories untold,
A tale of a hero whose nose got too cold.
He set out to conquer the great snowy peak,
But tripped on a snowball, oh, how unique!

Here in my fortress of pillows and fluff,
The warmth is inviting; I can't get enough.
But as I snuggle down for a cozy night's rest,
My cat steals the blanket, oh, what a jest!

Beneath the Snowy Canopy

Under the trees where the snowflakes fall,
I can hear them whisper, 'Come join the ball!'
Squirrels in twos host a wintertime dance,
While penguins in tuxes think it's their chance.

I tried to join in, but slipped on a patch,
And face-planted right in a snow-covered hatch.
Twirling and whirling like a snow globe gone mad,
My pals all still laugh, I'm the best they'll ever had!

Hot pie in the oven, it smells so divine,
But I'm catching my breath and missing my line.
I take one bite and burn my poor tongue,
Then laugh at the chaos, oh this is so fun!

The moonlight glows on the snowy expanse,
As I break out into my silliest dance.
Though the chill may bite, I'm warm in my heart,
With every giggle, I'm playing the part!

Frosted Moonlit Hues

Under the moon, the snowflakes dance,
Wearing jackets that are way too large.
They trip and giggle, what a chance,
To have a snowball fight at large.

The trees are dressed in ice so fine,
Like grandmas at a fancy ball.
Squirrels dashing, not a sign,
Of nuts around, they're bound to stall.

Each breath a puff, a cloudy plume,
While penguins try to sing their tune.
With every slip, there's room for gloom,
But laughter fills the frosty noon.

So grab a sled and take a seat,
We'll zoom down hills, oh what a feat!
With cheeks that ache from frosty heat,
We'll laugh until we're off our feet.

Whispers Between Snowflakes

Tiny whispers from the sky,
As snowflakes puff and float about.
They touch my nose, I start to cry,
It's so cold, I might just shout!

The penguins waddle with great flair,
In tuxedos made of frozen air.
They slide and hop, without a care,
While I just wish for summer's glare.

Every flake comes with a joke,
About a snowman's funny hat.
He lost his nose when it went broke,
Now he's a snowman—just like that!

So gather round the frozen lake,
We'll ice skate till our feet are sore.
With giggles and a silly ache,
We'll make snow angels, then want more.

The Language of Cold Winds

The chilly breeze has much to say,
It tickles ears and steals the hats.
In frozen jokes, the wind will play,
While dancing with the naughty cats.

A gusty warning, watch your back,
As frosty fingers pinch and poke.
Snowflakes fall in a giddy stack,
Making snow-dogs chase the smoke.

Icicles hang like big fangs sharp,
Beware the melt, oh what a plight!
As snowmen lean, they often harp,
About their dreams of summer light.

The cold winds laugh, they're in a bind,
With frosty breath and silly sighs.
They tell us spring is not far behind,
And soon the flowers will arise.

Shivering Twilight

As twilight comes, the shadows creep,
The snowmen huddle, tight and warm.
They whisper secrets while we sleep,
And snicker at the cold's alarm.

With frosty noses, kids explore,
Building forts that seem so grand.
The snowball flings, a playful chore,
As giggles spark across the land.

But oh! The wind just blew my hat,
It twirls away, I dash and zip.
A dance with snowflakes, how about that?
Making me laugh until I trip!

Now gathered 'round the fire's glow,
We share our tales of goofy falls.
With mugs of cocoa, onward we go,
For winter fables beat the hall.

When Frost Kisses the Pines

The trees wear coats of icy lace,
While squirrels slide with comic grace.
A snowman grins with a carrot nose,
But slips and falls—oh, how it goes!

The chilly air brings giggles loud,
As kids make angels, proud and loud.
A dog leaps high in frosty glee,
But lands headfirst—what a sight to see!

Hot cocoa spills, a marshmallow fight,
They laugh and shout, what pure delight!
The frost may bite, but joy is here,
With winter fun that brings warm cheer.

Shadows in a Crystal Landscape

The moonlight spills on frosty ground,
As penguins waddle round and round.
They slip and slide in silly ways,
Performing acts that earn loud praise!

Snowflakes dance like tiny bees,
Tickling noses with the softest freeze.
The trees wear hats, quite a sight to see,
Wobbling lightly—oh, what glee!

Icicles hang like crystal swords,
As snowmen pull some funny cords.
A snowball flies, a faceplant, too,
In this frosty world, laughter ensues!

Whispers of the Frostbitten Night

In the dark, the shadows play,
A raccoon sneezes—oh, what a day!
He hides his head in the snow so deep,
While the owls hoot and the crickets sleep.

The frost creates a world so bright,
But penguins breakdance out of sight.
A snowball fight leads to a truce,
With giggles echoing like a wild moose!

Under the stars, the critters cheer,
Making memories that we hold dear.
The whispers carried on icy breeze,
Tickle our hearts and bring us ease.

The Stillness of Icy Reveries

In quiet fields, the snowflakes fall,
They land on noses, ears, and all.
The polar bears play peek-a-boo,
As snow grips tight on the bright blue hue.

The silence bursts with laughter's sound,
As children build a fort so round.
A snowball hits a nearby tree,
Then rolls back down—what a funny spree!

The icy nights invite a dance,
While oddball creatures take a chance.
In frosty dreams, we giggle and sigh,
As stars twinkle in the midnight sky.

Heartbeats in the Chill

In the snow, my nose did freeze,
I danced around in frigid ease.
The snowman waved with carrot grin,
I tripped and fell, oh where to begin!

My hot cocoa's lost its charm,
It's just ice now, doesn't warm.
The sledges glide and giggles rise,
But one slipped cheek almost capsize!

With frosty breath, I shout and cheer,
The penguins wink and nudge me near.
Ice-skating ducks with floppy feet,
Make silly spins – oh, what a treat!

So let us laugh beneath this chill,
A cheeky flick, a snowball thrill.
The cold may nip, but spirits bright,
Make every moment sheer delight!

Solitude Beneath Winter's Gaze

On a frozen lake, I sit and muse,
The ice is thick; I might refuse.
Thoughts of cocoa start to dance,
But then I hear a snowball's chance!

Icicles hang like frozen teeth,
A squirrel winks, and I seize my wreath.
He scampers by in fuzzy glee,
While I just sip and watch his spree.

The frost has painted trees so white,
But see, that's where I lost my sight!
The sun peeks out, a teasing glow,
But it's my scarf that steals the show!

So here I sit, in quiet awe,
Of nature's pranks and gentle law.
In solitude, I find the jest,
Until the snowman claims the rest!

Fragments of Frost

Sprinkles of snow on my favorite cap,
Look at me — I'm quite the chap!
Each flake is different — who would've known?
But here am I, self-styled in cone!

The icy breeze whispers a tune,
I'm busting moves beneath the moon.
Frosty fingers twist and play,
While squirrels stare at my ballet.

'Join the fun,' the chill seems to say,
As I stumble, glide, and laugh away.
My nose is red, my cheeks are too,
But the snowy scene brings joy anew!

Each moment, a giggle, a slip or a slide,
Embracing the odd, with puffed-up pride.
In fragments of frost, we play and sing,
A winter's tale, what joy it brings!

The Poetry of Silence

In silence thick, with snow it waits,
A world transformed — it triggers fates.
But here I stand, boots all a-clop,
My quiet's gone, plop, plop, plop!

The crunch of snow beneath my feet,
Is like a song, a rhythmic beat.
But oh! What's that? A hare's mad dash,
He scared me silly — oh, what a crash!

Trees wear coats of frosted lace,
Yet somehow I lose my grace.
A dance with trees, I laugh and shout,
These are moments what life's about!

So let the world hush, let it snooze,
In sparkles bright, I cannot lose.
For in this chill, I find my smile,
The laughter warms, despite the trial!

Frost-Kissed Reverie

Snowflakes dance upon the nose,
Icicles hang like frozen toes.
Hot cocoa spills, a marshmallow dive,
Giggling in snow, we come alive.

Sleds fly down with squeaks and squeals,
Colder chills, but what fun feels!
Frosty breath like clouds on a leash,
Snowman dreams of a beachy feast.

The Secrets of Frozen Branches

Branches coat in icy shawls,
Birds wearing boots on frosty calls.
Squirrels slip, oh what a show,
Chasing tails in a frosty glow.

Pine cones slip, tree trunks wear hats,
Snowmen giggle where sunlight brats.
Nature's jesters in frigid play,
Winters' folksy, silly ballet.

Melodies of a Shivering Dawn

Dawn tiptoes in with chilly grins,
The sun yawns wide, then slowly spins.
Frosty whispers stir the air,
Snowflakes tumble like floppy hair.

A snowplow's tune, a grumpy hum,
As snowballs fly and mittens thrum.
Hot chocolate laughs in a cheerful mug,
While frostbit toes just want a hug.

Whispers Beneath the Ice

Beneath the sheets of icy glimmer,
Where frogs in sweaters plot and shimmer.
Chattering chips beneath the snow,
Secret parties 'neath the glow!

Snowballs whisper, 'Let's have a ball!'
Fuzzy mittens trapped in snow walls.
Teasing winds with playful bites,
Froggies dance in frosty tights.

Milton Keynes UK
Ingram Content Group UK Ltd.
UKHW022007131124
451149UK00013B/1044